TAKE BACK YOUR MOUNTAIN

Also by Jeff Hutchens:

Take Back Control: coach yourself to a 'stress-less' life
Take Back your Confidence: coach yourself to 'stress-less' confidence

TAKE BACK YOUR MOUNTAIN

Success and reflection from Everest Base Camp

Jeff Hutchens

Copyright © 2013 by Jeff Hutchens
ISBN: Softcover 978-1-291-43601-3

All rights reserved. No part of this book may be reproduced or transmitted in any form or by any means, electronic or mechanical, including photocopying, recording or by any information storage and retrieval system, without permission in writing from copyright owner.

This book was printed in the United States of America.

To order additional copies of this book, contact:
www.Lulu.com

CONTENTS

INTRODUCTION..9

PART ONE: TRAINING................................11
The Beginning...13
Embracing the rain and the 'swish'.....................14
Ice-running in Poland..15
Everest Goal Setting..16
The 'Tough Ten'..17
Pen y Fan..17
Minchinhampton..18
Ready for Heathrow...18

PART TWO: THE TREK TO EVEREST..........21
Kathmandu Bound...23
Heathrow..23
Kathmandu Domestic Airport.............................25
The Everest Trail...29
Trek One: Lukla to Phakding..............................29
The Purpose of the Trek to Everest.....................31
Trek Two: The Climb to Namche Bazar...............34
The Power of Positivity......................................36

Trek Three: Namche to Phortse..........................39
Trek Four: Phortse to Dongboche........................41
The Darkness of Dingboche..............................43
Overcoming Limiting Beliefs on the Everest Trail.......44
Developing Empowering Beliefs..........................45
Trek Five: Dingboche to Loboche........................47
NLP Tips for Controlling the Inner Dialogue............49
Visualisation..51
Trek Six: The Trek to Everest Base Camp................52
Trek Seven: Beginning of the End…Return to Orsho...55
NLP Presuppositions that supported me on the Everest Trail..56
Trek Eight: Back to Namche Bazar.......................58
Trek Nine: Lukla Again.................................60
The Size of your Thinking..............................62
Kathmandu Again..64
Following in the Footsteps of Others...................65
Peace in the Mountains?................................66
Future for Nepal.......................................68
Values Rediscovered on the Everest Trail...............71
The Return...72
Everest – The Mountain Analogy.........................73
Managing your State....................................74

PART THREE: THE AFTERMATH..............75
Reflections on my trip.................................77

What next?..77
Post script: Reflections from the Wenallt – Again........78
The Challenge..81

GLOSSARY OF TERMS...............................83
RECOMMENDED READING......................85

INTRODUCTION

> "To dream anything that you want to dream. That's the beauty of the human mind. To do anything that you want to do. That is the strength of the human will. To trust yourself to test your limits. That is the courage to succeed" Bernard Edmonds

It was time for adventure! I had achieved so much over the last few years – from my studies, my MA, running my marathons, and the writing of my first two books. But there is so much more out there – and what better place to start than climbing to the base of highest mountain in the world! The need for adventure had been growing for a while – and a trip to climb Kilimanjaro had already fallen through due to some difficult family circumstances last year. Finally, a few random conversations with work colleagues Aimi and Ellie regarding polar bears, the poles, a few huskies, and the mountains of the world led to the plan to climb to Everest Base Camp in 2013.

I began the training this year, and finally achieved one of the adventures of a lifetime this Easter. Of course, as a writer, I had ideas of a third book – and so what you have in your hand is an account of my adventure. It contains the literal and metaphorical ups and downs of the trek including the trials, difficulties, and triumphs on the Himalayas as I struggled with the most difficult thing I have done so far. The highs are the highest, and the lows are the lowest. It was such an experience – on that will live on in my memory.

As a coach, I have added the life lessons l learned – and of course put in some of the NLP theory behind the strategies that supported me on the mountain. I hope that it provides you with some insight into my adventure, but more importantly that it inspires you towards an adventurous life for yourself – whatever form that takes for you. I hope that you find the inspiration to Take Back your Mountain, and the live the life you always wanted – but up until now could only dream of. This book is about turning your dreams into reality and living your life for all that it is worth. I am sure that you will take up the challenge, and find your own adventures – I'm sure I will continue with you in the quest for more…

I have also included extracts from my diary and from the 'Bisco blog' which Aimi wrote to keep all of our families and friends up to date on the trek.

Aimi's Blog can be found in full at:

http://hutchschofandbisco.wordpress.com/

I hope that you enjoy reading as much as I have enjoyed reliving and recounting my story right here. It was the experience of a lifetime, and it taught me so much. I wish you all the best as you also 'Take Back your Mountain'.

Jeff Hutchens
May 2013

PART ONE: TRAINING

THE BEGINNING...

> "Today is life - the only life you are sure of. Make the most of today. Get interested in something. Shake yourself awake. Develop a hobby. Let the winds of enthusiasm sweep through you. Live today with gusto"
>
> Dale Carnegie

It is Boxing Day 2012, and I find myself trekking up the Wenallt just outside Cardiff – in the pouring rain!! What am I doing there? Well obviously I am starting my training for my climb to Everest Base Camp. At least it feels like I am starting my training, but in reality I have only had three weeks off running since I started back to it last July in Majorca where I ran most days - and even walked up a 500 step staircase from the beach around four times.

I am also on a nostalgia trip. The Wenallt is the hill (I think I used to refer to it as a mountain!?) that I spent much of my childhood in the days before parent paranoia took control of the world we now live in! To think that I would spend all day, every day, of my summer holidays – any holidays come to think of it – out of sight of my parents on a wild mountainside is quite a thought these days! Anyhow, nostalgic it is and I had great fun stretching my muscles *and* reliving the paths of my childhood – many of which are still there. It is also the place that I had been watching on the series 'Merlin' as I am convinced that I recognise half of the wood scenes as the back of the Wenallt! I was half expecting some encounter with an otherworldly being on my trek.

It is literally thrashing it down with rain, but I am more than equipped with waterproofs and boots so that I can really enjoy the climb. Well I say climb – but clearly I was much smaller in those days and so I find myself endlessly walking up and down, in an attempt for it to 'feel more like proper training' and so justify the time away from the family around Christmas! It's amazing how things change in nearly thirty years, and only some of them are my perspective! I used to go up the top of the Wenallt in my youth to 'gain some perspective' as I could see the whole of Cardiff from my vantage point. So I thought to do today - what better place than to do some goal setting for myself, and gain some vision for my future? Of course, thirty years is a long time in the life of trees!! The view is now completely obscured by thirty foot trees and no clear view of Cardiff is available – despite a number of attempts to find a different vantage point!

So now I'm in contemplative mode!! Perhaps my own life has become a little like this – where things were clear and straightforward when I was younger, now things have grown up in my life to complicate the view! Responsibilities, changed priorities, pressures, and expectations have taken the place of the clarity. Perhaps I am gaining some perspective after all!! Time to get my coaching head on and think through what is really important to me and what is really getting in the way of my enjoying the 'view' in my life.

This book is about taking back your 'mountain' and for me the main focus is about climbing Mount Everest, and following my adventure dreams. However, it perhaps also can become a metaphor for how I can 'take back' the 'mountains' of my childhood – and regain what I really value and find important in my life. It is time to get in to training mode – I am about to reclaim another mountain, as I climb Pen y Fan again, and perhaps a few other welsh peaks – and I am ready to claim back what is important to me in the process. 'Life's for the living – so live it, or you're better off dead!' is a mantra I came across by the singer Passenger, and so here is to discovering how to live it in the best possible way!! For me it means adventures and personal growth as an author and coach – what will it be for you?

> "Set a goal to achieve something that is so big, so exhilarating that it excites you and scares you at the same time" Bob Proctor

Embracing the rain and the 'swish'

I have a friend who loves running in the rain – in fact she prefers it, and I remember being shocked by this as we trained for the London Marathon back in 2011. I hate running in the rain, so imagine my joy when I am awoken a few days after Boxing Day to be informed by my wife that the 'weather isn't great' by which she meant it was throwing it down! Now having planned the day before to go out for my first run since Christmas, as a 'rain-hater' in Manchester this was not good news! I also realised that living in the UK, this was not going to gain me the year round fitness that I have set for one of my goals!

I then decided to change my thinking. With my NLP head on I decided to 'embrace' the rain. I too would become a 'rain runner' like my friend – I would dress appropriately and go out anyway. This I did, and felt all the better for it – just as I had battled the elements on Boxing Day – though the boots and waterproofs had seemed more fitting somehow!

I had embraced the 'swish' during my marathon training, and I now drew on this ability of mine to embrace things I naturally hated! The 'swish' is the sound of the water swishing around the bottle that I run with. I had a similar discussion with my friend during the marathon training – we both hated the sound of the water swishing around once you had taken your first swig. Now in order to run more than 10 miles it is necessary to carry a bottle, and so I had taken the plunge and learned to love the swish – I had embraced the swish!! And now I would embrace the rain in a similar manner!

If I think back long enough on my journey through life, drama teaching, running and coaching – I have long had an ability to embrace the unwelcome, the unknown, and the detestable!! From the times when I forced myself to 'enjoy' volunteering for improvisations during my Mime School days, through to standing in front of a variety of audiences in teaching all over the world – and more scarily, Hartcliffe in Bristol! I also was the one who would do anything to get out of what was then called 'cross-country ' in PE lessons – which was when the teacher hadn't planned a lesson so sent us all on a run around Llanishen estate for our 'fitness'. Since then I have run over 10 half marathons, a number of 10k races and of course the London Marathon – I have embraced running, and come to enjoy it! Remarkable!

In life - the ability to embrace and enjoy things I naturally hate has become a skill of mine, and I look forward to seeing what other things I will need to embrace in order to Take Back my Mountain…

Ice-running in Poland…

> "Successful people are successful because they form the habits of doing those things that failures don't like to do" Albert Gray

Sometimes I wonder about myself! Here I am on a school trip to Poland with some sixth form students to visit Auschwitz and Schindler's factory, and I am out running in the snow and ice at 6.30am!! Now *that* is commitment! I manage two runs in total over the four day visit – but what a lovely way to see Krakow! I am also walking around this beautiful city, and so the training is well and truly kicking in now. When I get back I face the 'Tough Ten' trail race in Weston Super Mare on Sunday morning – so I am desperate to keep my fitness up. I am secretly hoping that it is slightly misnamed, and it is only ten miles after all (I am trying not to think about the trails and the hills!).

Everest Goal Setting

For me the process of goal setting for my Everest trip was simple. I had a dream and turned it into a reality through planning and determination. The goal kept me through the difficult times – I had determined beforehand to succeed, so I did. When it got tough, I was determined to persist because I had set it as a goal. I chose to find the mental strength, the physical determination, and the drive to go beyond my limitations *because* I wanted to achieve my goal. I always had it in my sights.

A simple goal setting process:

- Dream big

- Set a goal – give the dream a deadline for achievement

- Make your plans for success

- Go and do it!

- Achieve your dreams...

A clearly defined goal:

- Stated in positive terms

- Owned by you

- Contributes to the common good of everyone affected

- Achievable in more than one way

The 'Tough Ten'

So a trail run in Weston, from the beach and into the hills for only ten miles wasn't really going to be hard was it? As it turns out there is nothing ironic about the name!! I had just returned from Poland – having run in the snow and ice a couple of times, and had very little sleep – and I had been quite moved by the experience at Auschwitz. It was a school trip and I had been on duty for four days, and lost a night's sleep somewhere – or it felt like it!

The 'Tough Ten' proved a bit of a challenge, and as it was over trail, wearing new trail shoes – a little too tight! After eight miles (and the second extreme hill) I was feeling burned out, and had to dig deep to even finish in 1h 35 (I wanted less than 1h 30….so not too bad) but my Achilles tendon has flared up and I find myself limping to the car. But I did it! At times like these – when the going gets hard – it is only the longer term goals that keep the short term in perspective. I have Everest in my sights – only three weeks away – and I will reach that goal.

Take time for your long term goals, as they make the short term do much more bearable when times get difficult! Coaching lesson here!!

Pen y Fan

Time for a mini-mountain at last! I have to test out whether the 'walking uphill' on the treadmill is actually doing me any good! We arrive at the car park around 10.30am and start our eight mile trail which involves climbing Cribyn, Pen y Fan and Corn Ddu, and should take around five hours.

It is truly a beautiful day, and before long we are stripping our layers as the climb up the side of Cribyn to 700m proves quite a challenge in the long grass. It is a relentless climb up the steep sides, and I find a will inside to just keep going. In my mind, I suppose I am climbing up Everest – and trying not to think that it is over 4000m higher than I am going today! I will do this mini-climb – and I will make it count. The views from the top of Cribyn, then Pen y Fan are stunning – and I wonder why I have never done this before. This is only just over an hour from my house, and I could literally do this every weekend! I need to spend more time in the mountains again!

Five and a half hours later, after some stunning scenery, lovely conversation, a random (?) meeting with Aimi's mum, and a whinging Achilles – and we are back. It is a lovely sense of accomplishment – and all of us are gearing up in our minds for the next hill climb, I'm sure. Yes, next time it will be Everest! Bring it on!

Learning point here: each new experience has its own challenge. This may not have been Everest, and is so small in relation to the real thing. Yet each one of us accomplished something today – and was an achievement in itself. I am happy to grow one step at a time. I can learn from each growth spurt out of the comfort zone. Yet I think the next challenge may be a bit of a step up!!

Minchinhampton

A gentle little 10k to get us in the mood for next weekend - how hard can it be? It is billed as part road, part trail – and we begin in the mud on the common in Minchinhampton! I am fit for the race, I know I am – but I think I am starting to feel weary from the constant training. Even before the race begins I struggle to stretch out my Achilles tendon, and after only a couple of miles it is throbbing. Not only that but my blister has developed as I over-compensate for the Achilles – and I am in agony for the last few miles of the race! I finish in just under an hour, and the limp is apparently quite noticeable by the end of the race! I am determined to be fit for Everest in a week, but this is starting to become a bit of a worry. I have done some real damage on the Tough Ten, and it isn't going anywhere soon by the looks of things. Joy!

> "Often the difference between a successful person and a failure is not one has better abilities or ideas, but the courage that one has to bet on one's ideas, to take a calculated risk - and to act" Andre Malraux

Ready for Heathrow…

So it's the day before – and I'm finally quite excited! I have been running – a lot! My Achilles is playing up, and I didn't think I was going to make it to the end of Michinhampton 10k – but I did. Now a week later and I think it will be ready for Monday – the first actual trek.

So I'm sat here, and have finally got round to browsing some photos of the Everest region. And now I am excited! It struck me other day that Nepal is in Asia! I know – obvious, but I was so focused on Everest that I failed to notice that I was also hitting another from my 'bucket list' of going to all five major continents before I die! How great to get two for one, and so I am double excited!

From a coaching point of view, I am finally hitting goals that have been embedded since I was on tour in the USA with a mime troupe, and a kind fella sat us down and got us thinking about our future legacy. Mike Stevens from Chicago should have a credit note at this point, because he took time out to make a difference in our lives as a troupe – and obviously is still having an impact in mine! Twenty two years later and I am about to climb Everest (well get to the bottom of it!), and travel east for the first time in my life!

Of course, this gets me thinking about the other continents, and I have been impressed recently with the 'coldest journey' that Sir Ranulph Fiennes and his group have planned across Antarctica - which he has had to pull out of due to frost bite – but which is imminent. I am not saying I will do it in winter – but I plan to travel there one day! Perhaps I should start planning when I return from Everest! But what about South America….and Australia…and I could go on!!

"Be daring, be different, be impractical, be anything that will assert integrity of purpose and imaginative vision against the play-it-safers, the creatures of the commonplace, the slaves of the ordinary"
Cecil Beaton

PART TWO:
THE TREK TO EVEREST

KATHMANDU BOUND!

> "To dream anything that you want to dream. That's the beauty of the human mind. To do anything that you want to do. That is the strength of the human will. To trust yourself to test your limits. That is the courage to succeed" Bernard Edmonds

Heathrow

I can't believe it, but the day has arrived. Today I fly to Kathmandu via Delhi, and set foot for the first time on the continent of Asia. Sometimes it takes a long time to fulfill your dreams (over twenty years in this case), but if they are real to you – then you will do it! I love this sense of achievement alongside the other parts of my adventure.

After a full day at school I am finally sitting at Heathrow having a last 'decent' meal, before the 12 hour journey to Kathmandu. I am so excited, I love airports anyway, but this time it seems on another level.

The flight itself is fairly uneventful, aside from two airplane curries and a couple of hours in New Delhi airport – and I arrive safe and sound at Kathmandu airport having missed a night's sleep. Suddenly it is four o'clock in the afternoon and I am queuing for my visa. The minutes turn into an hour and a half, and the worry starts to creep in – we are supposed to be at a meeting at the Kathmandu Guest House at five and we are missing it right now! Despite attempts to phone, nothing seems to work here and the frustration is mounting! If we don't get on the programme for our flights to Lukla tomorrow, then our whole trek is in jeopardy! I remind myself that from an NLP point of view, worrying is no use – but carry on anyway!

The journey to the Kathmandu Guest House (KGH) is an experience in itself! I had not experienced driving in Asia before, naturally, so was largely unprepared for the 'relaxed' attitude to lanes, rules, and general care and attention! Generally, it appears that you just drive in the direction you want to go, create a lane if one doesn't exist, turn across traffic, and use your horn as much as possible so that everyone else gets out of your way! It seems to work, and the traffic flows like liquid in a weird slow moving gel that weaves in and around itself. Remarkably there are few accidents, despite the road disappearing into a pile of rubble and building work, every so often. So now I know! Welcome to Asia!

> "Only as high as I reach can I grow, only as far as I seek can I go, only as deep as I look can I see, only as much as I dream can I be" Karen Ravn

Around 5.30pm we arrive at the KGH and finally meet up with our guide for the trek – the time we were given as we landed was actually fifteen minutes out, so we are not as late as we anticipated, and I hadn't taken into account the local attitude to timing! This is a much more 'relaxed' attitude, and we are on track for tomorrow. After a short meeting we arrange to meet up for a meal with our Guide – Damber (but you can call me 'D'!) – We check in to the KGH and familiarise ourselves with the shower room and the local cockroach! It is going to be an interesting trip!

It turns out that the 'worrying strategy' was a waste of time – how many times do you worry about what might go wrong, wasting your energy on a pointless cycle, only to find out that what you were worrying about doesn't come about! Even if the worst happens – worrying doesn't actually change a thing! I didn't know it but I would need reminding of this again in the next couple of days!

Extract from the 'Bisco Blog'

Aimi writes: Well, the good news is that we made it to Nepal! The first thrill was the sight of snowy mountain tops peeking through the clouds just before we came in to land. Kathmandu airport was manic, with an hour-long wait for visas and Jeff's emergency mug-shots for $5.

Nonetheless, they let us in to the country and we boarded a rickety van to take us into the city. The journey itself was an overwhelming reminder of the foundations of this pursuit. Kathmandu is an incredible city, but poverty lines the streets and the journey ahead of us took on a new focus from the moment we saw this first hand. We toasted our adventure with a cold bottle of 'Everest' beer (when in Rome…) and are now off to pursue an elusive restful night's sleep while mulling the aspirations and fears for the adventure now set clearly before us. Bring it on!

Kathmandu Domestic Airport

The morning after a lovely meal with Damber and the girls, I am up early – excited yet worried (there I go again!) about 'that flight'! I had seen the video of one of the most terrifying flights, as the plane attempts to land on one of the shortest runways in the world and facing into the mountain! I start to psyche myself up, having not slept very well with the noise and the cockroaches, and soon I am back on the roads in the gel of traffic to the airport.

> "Let no feeling of discouragement prey upon you, and in the end you are sure to succeed"
> Abraham Lincoln

To say the domestic airport is different to its international counterpart would be something of an understatement! We sit to wait in amongst the chaos and lack of obvious queues (how we British love a queue!), and wonder how we will ever get to the right place. Damber had told us of the backlog of flights from the last few days – but hoped that our flight would go out. This had not been reassuring, but we presumed now the weather had improved that we would be fine. Two hours later we were back in the car and on our way to the KGH.

It was a bit of a shock and severe anti-climax to be sat once again in the meeting point at the KGH discussing the possible alternatives to our Everest Base Camp trip if the plane didn't fly tomorrow. It was a devastating blow! I had planned for this, trained for this, alongside taking into account all the people who had supported and sponsored us to do this! I tried to imagine what we would tell them: That we went to Kathmandu for two weeks? That we went for a trek in the Annapurna's? That we failed to get to Base Camp? I have worries that I won't cope physically, or with the altitude – but to not even get to Lukla to start my trek; this was beyond my comprehension.

To say the disappointment set in is an understatement, and as we went to lunch to experience the delights of a 'Dal Bhat' curry it was with heavy hearts in the extreme. Now the worry really set in! What if we didn't get to go at all? I tried telling myself that it was pointless to worry, but it didn't help! As a group we knew we had to stay positive – but it was hard, facing the very real possibility that our trek was over before it had begun.

At our second meeting that day, around 5.00pm, we tried to state as clearly as possible our case for having to fly tomorrow. We pleaded to get on the earliest flight – the earlier flights seem to have a better chance of going than the later ones. Eventually we were given some reassurance that they would try and get us on the 9.30am flight – the second one of the day (our flight, the third had been cancelled the day before) so we had to just hope that the second would go out. I think it was the mix of the missing the night's sleep, the worry and frustration over the fights, and three hot curries in two days, but at this point my tummy decided that its first battle of many this trip with food would take place – I would start my trek tomorrow on empty at best!!

> "Every adversity, every failure, every heartache carries with it the seed on an equal or greater benefit"
> Napoleon Hill

I write in my diary 'So I'm in Kathmandu and of course I decide to have a bout of 'Delhi Belly just to prepare me for my Everest climb! Great way to start what is probably the greatest challenge of my life! I guess it's the mix of two airplane curries, a poor steak, a missed night's sleep and the disappointment of not flying to Lukla. It is time to dig deep and get myself into recovery mode for a grueling trek to Everest Base Camp'

Extract from the 'Bisco Blog'

Aimi writes: The journey to the airport was a quiet one as we all tried to overcome the fear of 'that flight' whilst bracing ourselves for the physical challenge waiting for us the moment we landed. It turned out the toilets in the domestic terminal were a far more terrifying prospect…The wait for the flight was a long and nervous one, though Aimi did manage a brief nap lying on her rucksack in the middle of the terminal. Several crosswords later, a bleak white paper sign emerged through the bustling crowds at the check in desk: 'ALL LUKLA FLIGHTS DELAYED'. The devastation was difficult to hide and the eventual announcement of cancellation brought with it a wave of sadness. Suddenly, the only thing more terrifying than the prospect of getting on that scary plane was not getting on it.

Keeping our chins firmly up, we returned to Kathmandu to make a new plan. After recharging with the local speciality of dal baht and with a bit of a 'don't mess' attitude, we managed to secure seats on an earlier flight for tomorrow. Please keep everything crossed that the wind subsides for us (statement of the day from D: 'the planes are small and they dance when it is windy'.) All being well, this doesn't change our plans too greatly as we are cutting the expedition shorter by not taking an acclimatisation day in Namche Bazaar. This will make the trek tougher and the ferocity of the altitude harder to bear, but we are resolved to get the job done.

THE EVEREST TRAIL

Trek One: Lukla to Phakding

I am finally on the plane to Lukla after a day's delay, along with the possibility that all of the planes might be cancelled. It was a horrible time wondering if I would even get to start my adventure, worrying about the impact on the charity money and our friends and families responses back home. Again I am noticing the futility of worrying! It really had no bearing on the situation, and contributed nothing to help me out!

It is hard to describe the mix of excitement and slight trepidation that is setting my heart pacing. I feel like a kid on a roller coaster – excited, yet scared, thoughts of the fragility of the airplane and the tiny landing strip the other end. I put aside the memories of the same plane that crashed less than a year ago where everyone lost their lives that day. I can see similar expressions on the faces of Ellie and Aimi. But I am actually on the plane, and we are doing this! Sometimes you don't appreciate what you have until it is under threat – and I have never been more grateful to be on a plane in my life, even on this dangerous flight! You don't know what you have until you (nearly) lose it!

> "Enthusiasm releases the drive to carry you over obstacles and adds significance to all you do"
> Norman Vincent Peale

As I glance out of the window, once we reach the mountains, everything changes. I can see the tips of the snow-capped mountains joining us above the clouds, and I am reminded how often our dreams and goals take us above the clouds into new territories in our lives. This is where life out of the comfort zone begins – and that is where the fun starts!

I am starting my adventure for real – I am going to Everest Base Camp. The flight is so stunning, and I totally buzzing with excitement every moment as the incredible scenery unfolds – I love my mountains at the best of times, but this is something else! Everything seems new and special – like it was made just for my eyes today! The views are amazing, and I am totally engulfed by the mountains, everywhere I look there is a new summit surpassing the last. I love being here. I am in Asia and surrounded by some of the most amazing parts. I am also experiencing

Nepalese culture, but also about to begin trekking in amongst the world's highest mountains! Who gets to do this normally? Yet here I am – and loving it! I am achieving my goals.

Before I know it we have landed – the pilot gets an obligatory round of applause – and I have been introduced to our porters by the guide. The flight wasn't anywhere near the trauma that was anticipated, in fact I really enjoyed the excitement (just like a roller coaster with wings!), and I am reminded again about the needless worry I had over the flight.

Next thing I know we are trekking in the sunshine, learning to take things very slowly. Although I can't feel any difference yet I am now at 2800m, higher than I have ever been in my life whilst not in the air! The privilege of actually being here has given me so much energy, and I walk with a spring in my step, as gratitude creates an elation and joy that we are finally on our way. Gratitude is a powerful emotion; I should remember this for my coaching and teaching!

The views are spectacular on every twist and turn along the way – it is so hard to describe, but my love of landscapes, mountains, rivers and valleys is being satisfied and at the moment I am constantly surrounded by 6000m mountains, and beyond them I can already see the snow-capped peaks of the higher mountains ranges starting to appear. These are what Damber describes as 'real mountains' – apparently the others are just 'big rocks'! Albeit that they are three times the size of the highest peaks I have previously encountered in Wales and Scotland! I am humbled by this thought – and the adventure is only just beginning. Soon I will be amongst the highest, and living my dream!

> "Patience, persistence and perspiration make an unbeatable combination for success"
> Napoleon Hill

The trek to Phakding is around five hours, ending at an altitude of 2,600m (technically we are going down at the moment), and the journey is largely flat with the occasional climb up and down as we traverse the valley side. It is a nice gentle ease in to the ten day trek, but already my Achilles tendon is playing up. I have had problems with this since the 'Tough Ten' in Weston a month ago, and as menioned it was very painful by the end of the Minchinhampton 10k. I have to make a decision here – I have ten more days of trekking, and I am determined to succeed. I have to start a little NLP mind battle with myself. Can I convince myself that pain is 'in the mind'? I decide to use a Miles Hilton-Barber technique – I imagine that my mind isn't in when it gets the call from my nerves – no-one at home just leave a message! I need all of my determination to see things through when the going gets tough – and it's tough already! This for me is mind over matter, and I ignore the fact that this is going to be triggered all the more when the inclines increase over the next few days.

The trail traverses the river valley a number of times, we are told that this river descends all the way from Everest Base Camp, and this adds to its significance for us somehow. It is time for myself and Ellie to face one of our fears – the wire bridges that criss-cross the river of which we will become very familiar. Ellie is admitting to her fear openly, and I have decided to try the 'acting confident' trick from my NLP training – nevertheless I am secretly relieved when Ellie asks that we do the first one hand in hand to support each other, and it turns out to be not such a big deal for me as I thought. I have this dilemma, you see – I love the water, particularly the sound of rushing water like we are crossing, and so a part of me wants to stand and watch, listen and feel a part of it (my inner hippy!?), and it seems useful to listen to this part of me at this time. I am reminded from NLP that choice is extremely important and that we always have one – particularly when choosing your attitude to a challenge. I decide to choose a positive attitude (not for the first or last time) this trip.

The Purpose of the Trek to Everest...

A sense of purpose gives meaning to your life. It is the stuff of passion – it is a reason to be here, to do what you want to do, and become who you want to be. I felt a huge sense of purpose once I had set the goal to climb to Everest Base Camp. It started to drive me, affected my training, and has affected my attitude from the inside out. But I also re-discovered something of a lost purpose for my life – and this has affected me more than the initial purpose I had for the trip. I love that!! I have found that my life is more than my career and this has changed me so much. I have also rediscovered the importance of making sure my career fits in with my overall purpose in life – and the change is ongoing!

What is it for you? What is your purpose? Are you living according to your life purpose? Will you make the changes you need for a purposeful life?

After a slow five hours of trekking we arrive in Phakding, and although it has yet to be too strenuous and I am still feeling tired and ready for a rest. I am then informed that we will go hiking in half an hour – just a short walk up 200m to a Primary School! It will take about ¾ hour!

The idea here is that we ascend above the altitude we are staying for the night, so that when we descend from the hike we are acclimatising ourselves ready for the next day. By the end of six days these would become very familiar – but the ascent is steep, harsh and I am breathless by the time I reach the top after only half an hour! I get the first sensation – which will also become familiar – of feeling like I've added 30 years to my life and get a glimpse of slow out of breath walks that remind me of my grandmother! It is a bit of a shock, but by the time I arrive back at the Tea House in Phakding, I am already feeling the benefit returning to a lower altitude.

> "Great dreamer's dreams are never fulfilled, they are always transcended"
> Alfred Lord Whitehead

This idea of 'going further' to grow your comfort zone represents the ideal of the whole trip for me. I believe this way of stretching yourself, so that you can achieve more within your comfort zone is an important principle. It encompasses the ideas of growth, stretching yourself, expanding your comfort zone, and going the extra mile. It is perhaps one of the main reasons that I push myself beyond my limits occasionally, so that life in comparison is extremely achievable. There is an important self-coaching principle here – always go further than you need, and enjoy the benefits later.

Later in the evening I get my first glimpse of the 'orange menu' laminated for resilience that will come to represent my biggest challenge. For now, blissfully unaware, I order my evening meal two hours ahead of time, and settle in to my room – which despite being extremely cold already has an 'en-suite' toilet (with a seat and flush like a 'real' toilet! These will soon become a distant memory…).

Extract from the 'Bisco Blog'

Aimi writes: Distracted by the whispering, bird-like shadow of our plane drifting over hillsides, the runway at Lukla was upon us before we knew it. Ellie was seated above the back wheels and felt these make contact with the concrete at the precipice of the mountain runway. How that plane landed so simply is beyond our comprehension.

A carb-fuelled breakfast at Lukla, and we were on our way; the very first steps of our ascent to Base Camp. The walk was rocky, green and truly beautiful. After braving a few rickety suspension bridges and yak-cow encounters, the stony walls of Phakding began to emerge over the horizon. We followed the last few steps of the trail, teetering above a rushing turquoise river, and reached our base for the night.

The anxiety of the last 48 hours has been exhausting, but our purpose here has been renewed. There is now gratitude in every step taken.

Trek Two: The Climb to Namche Bazar

It is another warm day, so the shorts are still on – and I am wondering if I packed too many 'cold weather' clothes which my pack is jammed with. Thankfully I only have my small day pack, with my standard two litres of water for the trek. It is very much a morning of criss-crossing the river again – in fact there are five bridges to circumnavigate, and my resolve to love the bridge views and sounds is imperative. The trek is starting to climb with each step now and the up and down to each bridge is starting to test my thigh muscles. I had no idea what was coming!

> "Difficulties are meant to rouse, not discourage. The human spirit is to grow strong by conflict"
> William Channing

After trekking for a good few hours we stop to allow a ridiculous amount of Yak/cows and donkeys to cross the final bridge in front of us. I begin to feel extremely frustrated at the amount of time we are stuck here – later I would begin to notice that a long steep climb would follow every time we stopped beyond the usual couple of minutes. The afternoon climb to Namche Bazar is a two and a half hour climb – straight up! Yes, we zigzag – but it is almost vertical as we gradually make our way up to the 3400m town. If I felt like a pensioner before – now I feel as unfit as I've ever felt, and I begin to question my training! I have to be reminded of how much I have done, and that no matter what – nothing could properly prepare anyone for ascending at altitude, other than actually doing it. And here I am actually doing it! One foot in front of the other – one step at a time. I begin to form a kind of mantra in my head, and I use it each day of the trek from now on: "One foot in front of the other. Up, up, up. Slowly, slowly. It's all about the climb".

It is here that my NLP positive thinking and mind psychology becomes really important. I tell myself that it is 'all about the climb': I am here to climb to Base Camp after all! I tell myself that 'I didn't come here to walk down hills'! I start to smile at the ascents – and to decide my attitude is to enjoy them. The mind is so powerful in this – and it literally makes all the difference to my trek to Everest Base Camp. More of that later! When it comes to trekking at altitude, slow and steady is the only way to go – it literally minimises altitude sickness. Pacing yourself is essential, as in life! And I learned that just when you think you can't make it, if you dig deep then you can always find something else inside yourself. When you think you have given your all – you always have just that little more to give, even for just one more 'hike' after a day's hard trek.

> "I had rather attempt something great and fail, than to attempt nothing at all and succeed"
> Robert H. Schuler

Needless to say the views were getting ever more spectacular – each time we turn another corner, round another bend we are rewarded with ever more breathtaking scenery. My first sight of Everest is naturally significant – even though it is merely the tiniest tip over the other mountains far in the distance. I just know that my goal is finally in sight, and it will become ever clearer as the days past. This is really happening and I am doing this – and I can see the top of the world! I am loving this – despite the complaining muscles – I am really on my way to Everest and it's fantastic.

There are so many beautiful views, the kind I would buy if on a poster – yet they are all around me! I just have to look up to appreciate them. For much of the trekking you have to look at your feet, from a safety point of view – and it is so easy to get bogged down in the minutiae of the walk. But the views are there if only I can stop occasionally and look up. I am reminded that in life – how often I get bogged down in the small details – it pays to look up occasionally and get perspective from the bigger picture! A new perspective can change so much – and I am getting one at every turn on this journey.

I can see the girls are equally moved as we continue our ascent to Namche – and all of us are relieved to round the final corner and see the brightly coloured buildings of Namche appear on the side of the mountain above us and we walk up step after step into the town to get to our next Tea House. We are soon out hiking up to a nearby museum and some Buddhist monuments, then back to have our last shower for a week! Yes, as Damber had promised: "After Namche we are all smelling like Yaks!" (It would be much later we would discover that he had not showered for two months!)

The Power of Positivity

A positive, 'can do' attitude underpins the whole of NLP. It is a winning attitude and it is infectious. A positive attitude is also a choice. What will you choose today?

A positive attitude is linked with self-belief and a solutions focus. A person with a positive attitude is a person who will get things done. It is not a blind optimism – it is an attitude that is linked with the persistence and determination to succeed. It is a positive work ethic that recognises the effort that needs to be made – and then gets to it! It is about remaining motivated.

Positivity is linked with a vibrant love of life that is a conscious state of mind. The Costa Rican call it 'pura vida' which literally translated means 'it's a great life!' I am reminded of the LG adverts – life is good! Remember that you get what you expect – what characterises you? What are you expecting?

I love being known for my positivity! On the trail Damber would often check with us by asking 'Thik chha' (pronounced 'chi cha') meaning 'Are you okay?' It meant that he knew we were coping with the altitude and were ready for the next challenge on the trail. I would always reply yes, but once I decided to use my given nick name and replied 'Sham is Thik tha', and I heard Damber giggle and reply 'Yes, Sham is always Thik chha.' I was so chuffed! For me it was recognition for my positive mindset, and that it was noticeable. Aimi had already picked up on my 'Chirpy chirpy' song which I subconsciously did from time to time.

It is great to be known as a positive person – and I hope that it is infectious and always noticeable. I also believe that it will stand me in good stead for the all the challenges that lie ahead for me. What are you characterised by? What do you want to be known for? What is infectious about you – what are people catching from you?

Give yourself time for a positive review of the day – what went well? Start looking for what works rather than looking for the negative – it is an excellent way to realise how successful you are. Start with your positivity today. Are you ready?

> "It always seems impossible until it is done"
> Nelson Mandela

I am thinking of how so often our goals need a little sacrifice as part of the process of their fulfillment – ask yourself: "What will I sacrifice in order to achieve my goal?" Is it simply home comforts such as toilets, showers and edible food – as in this trek for me? Well, alongside the sacrifice my muscles, lungs and stomach were going to make on my behalf (I still had no idea how tall and hard the 'wall' was going to be for me!). What about you? What will you sacrifice in the short term to get what you really want in the long term? What is really important for your life?

At Namche I am at 3400m and I realise that I am starting to get affected by the altitude. My increasing shortness of breath on the climbs, the mild headaches and dizziness, and now the palpitations are all part of this. I am not worried, but have a quiet word with Damber, and he assures me that this is part of it, but it is very mild – if I take it slowly, things should be fine. Of course, he has already given us a few tales of the death of people who ignore the symptoms and proceed regardless – but I try to put this out of my mind.

I write in my diary: "I am coping with it but I clearly have mild AMS (Acute Mountain Sickness), but I am determined to get there and back. I wish the palpitations would stop, but I am reassured that my resting heart-rate is only 66. I think I am fit enough, but I am feeling my age. I think I have had a glimpse of old age – the slow walk is essential up here."

> "Perseverance is failing 19 times and succeeding the 20th."
> Julie Andrews

I begin a battle which will climax at Loboche with the altitude and my worries over whether I will actually make it to Base Camp. There is an unspoken agreement that we are in this together, and none of us wants to be the one who sabotages the trip with altitude problems. I note the pressure start to build about my own state, and wonder if I am the weak link in the team. This part of the psychological battle to claim my mountain is something I had not really accounted for before and it would become a big part of the victory I would achieve in the end.

Extract from the 'Bisco Blog'

Aimi writes: Today was tough. The sun was beating and there was a great height to climb, but we have made it to Namche Bazaar. Another porridge breakfast and we were on the trail by 8am. The morning was relatively easy going and involved several more rickety wire suspension bridges. With the river charging below you and the wind blowing prayer flags over your path, there is nowhere to look but straight ahead.

We stopped for a very early lunch before 11am as this was to be our last opportunity to eat before Namche. A bowl of noodles and we were walking again and the walk soon got tough. The ascent to Namche was delayed by a few dozen donkeys meandering over the final bridge but, after a minor water bottle explosion, we started the steep rocky zig-zag climb. It was a long time to be climbing hard in the blazing sun, but we were rewarded by our first sight of the elusive peak of Mount Everest. Eventually we saw the coloured roof-tops of Namche from across the valley and knew that our challenge for the day was almost complete. We arrived at the tea house with a lingering sense of disbelief. Day two: job done.

A quick cup of tea and then it was time for a 'short hike'. It is becoming increasingly evident that these 'short hikes' are the toughest part of our day. We climbed around 400m in just over an hour (this means steep) to a very big rock. Every step was a little wobblier than the last and recovery breaths became increasingly harder to summon as the air thinned at nearly 3800m.

Trek Three: Namche to Phortse

> "The major reason for setting a goal is for what it makes of you to accomplish it. What it makes of you will always be the far greater value than what you get" Jim Rohn

The seven hour trek to Phortse is a day of relentless up and down, along the tiniest of mountain paths that involved constant re-iteration of my inner mantra. Just keep going, up and down, slowly and surely one step at a time. The growing fatigue in my muscles has kicked in and my body is starting to hate me!

The journey involves many views of a growing Everest tip beyond the mountains, spectacular views of the contrasting mountains we were walking around and the dramatic cliff sides dropping down into the river valley – now far below. For me, it is very much time to face my fear of heights head on. I am not really great with heights, and I just have to bear it in my job at a variety of times when at the top of a ladder rigging lights or staging. This is something else! Each time we pause to look at more wildlife on the sides of the cliff above dramatic drops of around 500m, I tend to cling to the back side of the path, as Damber places himself at the edge on the smallest of rocks!

It gets easier as dealing with your fears head on inevitably is, and I survive having grown just a little more! Going down the steep climbs proves as traumatic as the continuous climb – and after my first 'fall', into the icy mud (yes pleasant sight on my backside – and yes it *was* that colour!!), I am more than a little wary of the inclines. Calamity Jeff (or Sham, as I had now been named by my guides who struggled with our English names!), had struck again – did I forget to mention bashing my head on the low outside toilet doorframe on the first day!!?? I am reminded that in life one step at a time is important, and sometimes as MLK stated: "You only need to see the first step on the staircase" to make a start on your journey to achieve your goals.

> "If you know what to do to reach your goal, it's not a big enough goal"
> Bob Proctor

At Phortse there is yet another climb for acclimatisation up to a monastery this time, and only a short hike of about ¾ hour, and I am soon drying off my stinky shorts, and ready to start trying the 'squat' toilets! Another glance at the dreaded laminated orange menus after tea to order the morning porridge, and I head to a freezing bedroom in the latest Tea House. Home comforts seem a long way away, as I trudge to the outside toilet at five in the morning – but the early view of the mountains is once again spectacular. I hope I don't get used to this, and stop appreciating where I am. I am nearing the top of the world, and I want to love every minute of it. Nevertheless I rush back to the relative comfort of my 'Everest down' sleeping bag. What a great buy for 3900m freezing temperatures!

Extract from the 'Bisco Blog'

Aimi writes: The further we climbed the more the mountain tops rose above the horizon. We are running out of euphoric adjectives to describe the scenery now, but it was awesome. Views of mountains were panoramic and Everest, though more prominent today, almost faded into insignificance behind its dominant peers in closer proximity to our path. These powerful mountains are humble in their search for limelight, but are only a hundred or so metres shy of Sagarmartha herself. Sagarmartha is the Sherpa name for Everest, literally meaning 'head of the sky'.

At 3900m, the sleepy Sherpa village of Phortse came into view. This was our stop for the night (a variation on our original itinerary, but further from the beaten track). As we clambered up to our tea house we walked past dozens of Sherpa women hard at work on their farmland. On arrival at the tea house, we were given a cold bucket of water to wash in before setting off for another short walk.

It really was brief today. We climbed to a secluded monastery and caught sight of some very cute baby yaks and enormous snow pigeons en route. The cloud quickly clambered into the valley and brought with it a, now familiar, sub-alpine chill. A quick return then to lots of warm layers, a hot dinner and a good night's sleep. The inevitable blisters, chapped lips and sunburn (even factor 50 sun block doesn't rescue you) are now becoming faithful friends and our nightly routine is one of careful preservation. Tomorrow the path leads to Dingboche.

Trek Four: Phortse to Dingboche

The journey to Dingboche started with a steep climb, and then more of the up and down that I am becoming accustomed to although my body is starting to get weary. I am generally feeling okay – thik-chha ('chi cha') – but I am weary to my bones, and as I reflect on another seven hours of trekking, I note that I am struggling with the altitude at times.

I feel so unfit despite my training, but if I have AMS (Acute Mountain Sickness) then it is very mild. This is my fourth day of walking around seven or eight hours a day but I am coping and I am determined to make it.

> "If I have the belief that I can do it, I shall surely acquire the capacity to do it even if I may not have it at the beginning"
> Mahatma Gandhi

I am overcoming challenges each day, and at times I have to force each step through sheer determination – a test of mental toughness as well as the physical strain. I am pleased to be achieving my goals, and dealing with other fears along the way – such as my fear of heights as I trek along tiny paths with a 600m drop into the river valley below. My little 'calamities' over the last days have done little to boost my confidence over my footing on these treacherous paths.

I have been dealing with my damaged Achilles tendon, and with that I have good and bad days – and this one with the constant up and down, plus the rocky paths is proving to be a bad one. I am choosing to ignore the pain, as well as the added bonus of a plethora of blisters on my feet. After all I am a runner and so used to running on sore blisters. I can't let little things like this get to me – so the message is 'pain is in the mind' and therefore ignorable!

> 'It is not the mountain we conquer but ourselves'
> Sir Edmund Hilary

I was cold for the first time on the trek and as we passed through the bleakness of the Orsho I realise that I wasn't prepared for today – it is time to start testing out the 'cold' gear that I invested in.

My mind is in an interesting place, and I feel the constant testing of my resolve. The elation of being here has been replaced by a determination to succeed. It is starting to sink in how much of a challenge this trek is going to be. It feels a long way from Lukla, but the sight of the mountains that I am engulfed by is a constant re-energiser, along with the sight and sound of the river below. The local people are also inspiring in a different way – their contentment with a simpler way of life is a message in itself. I notice the children playing with homemade toys like from some 1950's documentary, and they seem satisfied to amuse themselves for hours with random bits of detritus from the street. I suppose it's the challenge of brushing with a developing country that raises questions of the complication of western life.

Extract from the 'Bisco Blog'

Aimi writes: It's fair to say, we are now reaching our porridge threshold. The days were starting to blur together this morning and we set foot on the trail feeling both far from home and a long way from our destination. The first part of the trail was fairly comfortable and we were excited by the sight of a group of tahr (a kind of Himalayan mountain goat), not far from our path .Before long the ascent became a lot more brutal and our legs and lungs were as heavy as lead. A brief tea stop and a quick snack to refuel were a necessary part of a long morning of walking.

As we kept on for another two or three hours a thick fog began to creep through the valley behind us and soon, the mountain tops had vanished. We were both above and below the cloud. The rapid ascents and descents were relentless and it was hard to comprehend that the altitude at lunch was not much higher than our summit on the previous day. We can't help feeling a little sense of pride in what our bodies are willing to do for us. As our rest stop for the night came into view, we raised our heads optimistically to D's call of 'short hike' and a chorus of 'jam-jam' (let's go) was heard as we trooped a further 150m up the hillside to acclimatise at 4550m. We are very conscious that the level of oxygen in the air is now only 60% of that at sea level, but we are still smiling.

The Darkness of Dingboche

I think it is safe to say that I have hit the 'wall' of my trek. I am feeling increasingly unwell, and the girls have had some food poisoning which has left Ellie feeling weak and fragile. I think this has forced me to face my sickness a little more head-on, and I am feeling vulnerable for some reason. It has hit me that we might not make this – and I had always presumed that it would never be an issue. I don't want to fail to reach my goal, and I think all of us are feeling that we daren't be the weak link that sends us home. It is providing another immense pressure alongside everything else.

> "There are no short cuts to any place worth going"
> Beverly Sills

I write in my diary 'I am really struggling today, having no messages from home I feel totally estranged. I saw an internet café whilst on our small acclimatisation hike (only three hours today as this is our 'day off'!), and thought of some possible contact with home and actually burst into tears. This is so not like me, and I think I need to dig deep for some emotional determination too. Deep down I know I can do this, but as my body struggles, my mind and emotions are more vulnerable I suppose.'

I needed to take control and so looked to my coaching ideals – I choose each step, literally saying 'yes', and embracing the hardships and struggles. I have chosen to come here, and as I walk through the 'wall' – mentally, physically and emotionally – I am finding new levels of determination I didn't know I had.

I am struggling to eat much at all. My appetite has all but disappeared, but I know I must for the energy I need. I am trying to drink enough, but I have that strange feeling of dehydration and yet over full and bloated that I last felt during the London Marathon in 2011. I have to find ways through this just like I did back then. I almost gag at the sight of a laminated orange menu, and the mere thought of food is triggering reflexes in my stomach. So lunch is a case of forcing a bowl of noodle soup down one mouthful at a time like it is poison!

Overcoming limiting beliefs on the Everest Trail

Limiting beliefs can sabotage your goals from the inside out if you let them, and keeping your mind focused and positive can make all the difference. The important thing when faced with limiting beliefs, fears and negative attitudes is to face them head on.

It is essential to realise that your thoughts are powerful. They create feelings, and these feelings influence how you live – they affect your capability. If you think you can't, you don't feel confident, and you produce a cycle of failure. The opposite is also true. Everything starts with a thought; your job is to control your thoughts to create the life you want.

I found this out so quickly at Dingboche. My mind started telling me that I was too ill to carry on, the girls getting sick allowed me to entertain the possibility that we wouldn't make it – and my thoughts started whizzing around my head. I call it the 'What if?' syndrome, as your mind finds all the possible negative consequences. I had to stop my thinking in my tracks and remind myself why I had come. When I started up the trail on our hike I started to consciously choose each step – focusing my thoughts on the choice with literally each step, I even recited 'choose' with each step until I began to embrace the challenge once more. It was vital in the silence of the hike along the trail to find positive things to fix my mind on, and my little mantras really helped.

Choose to think differently, replace the negative thinking with positive choice, and control that 'inner voice' so that it tells you what you need to hear. If the negative is overwhelming, find the volume dial and turn it down for a while. You are able to control your thoughts – they are yours!

NLP calls this 'reframing' where you choose to find a new way of looking at a situation – many call this giving it a 'positive spin'. You are literally choosing to think differently, to view the scene with new eyes, and changing your perspective on the situation. It is helpful to realise here that problems exist only in the mind – outside there are only sets of circumstances that you may respond positively or negatively to.

On the mountain I had to get my mind in order, to get my thinking straight. It was such a tough challenge, that my mind could have sabotaged the whole trip for me. My body will just go on – one step after another – I found that out. My mind was where the battle was won: choosing to ignore the pain, the aches, the sickness and the strange sensations; choosing to embrace the challenge, to positivity, the possibility that I could and would succeed.

The hike to 4800m today gave me feelings of hyperventilation and I am really starting to struggle for breath when climbing. I write in my diary: 'This is so much harder than I thought it would be – but I want to make it to EBC. This has been the hardest day despite only a short walk for a little over three hours'.

Developing Empowering Beliefs

Once you have overcome any limiting beliefs, you need to replace them with empowering beliefs. If you believe you can, you will find a way.

When you value something enough, you will find the empowering beliefs you need to make it happen. Empowering beliefs encourage you to take control of your life and you become responsible for the change you want. As Ghandi said 'You must be the change you want to see' and you must become responsible to make a difference in your life.

For me, I valued the adventure, valued the chance to climb to Base Camp enough to create an empowering belief for myself. I wanted to, needed to believe that I could do it – and I did! I put in the energy to make this come true.

What about you? What do you value enough to change your beliefs for? What will make you take responsibility for your life? What is your mountain?

The afternoon brings new hope as I finally get messages from home. I realise that Emma and Lisa *have* been reading our blog, and they reply to one or two of the posts. This leaves me feeling overwhelmed with emotion – but this time it is tears of joy of the connection to my family back home. This is quite a shock to my system and I start to plan a day with the family the Sunday I get back – but that is still a long way off, ten days, and I am just over half way through my climb let alone the journey back. However, the emotional boost is accompanied by a sight of the sun breaking through the clouds to bring a little light to the darkness of this place. I shall be glad to leave tomorrow.

I return to the freezing room that has been mine for the two days. Ironically, it has the best views yet – that of the 'twins' mountains I have seen from all sides by now as the trek progresses, and settle down to reflect on my day. I am learning so much about myself and despite the growing hardship; I am so pleased to be taking on this challenge.

Extract from the 'Bisco Blog'

Aimi writes: Before going to sleep last night, we were hit with a wave of food poisoning. Having made the mistake of ordering cheese for lunch, our bodies folded last night and it became impossible to keep anything down, even water. Forcing down some dry toast, we all felt nervous about the prospect of today's hike with energy stores exceptionally low. Nonetheless, we dragged on our walking boots and set foot on the trail. It was tough. Initially we had planned to scale the snowy hillside for a view of an expansive alpine lake at 5000m. However, the ice and our wobbly legs were against us, so we adjusted our route for a slow and rocky ascent to 4800m.

The walk was a silent one and each of us had to dig deep to find the motivation for the next step. Before long, we were descending back to Dingboche with reflections whirring through our minds. The thought of not reaching our goal was enough to push each of us deep into our reserves. We knew it wouldn't be easy. We knew it would hurt. Now it is just grit, determination and mental strength that will get us there. At times like this, your mind inevitably drifts to loved ones who feel so very far away. It now feels so important to recognise that in two days time we will reach our goal. From then every step taken will be a step towards home.

Trek Five: Dingboche to Loboche

It is with a new found lightness in my step that I leave behind the darkness of Dingboche, and I the sun heralds a bright new start to the day. Once again we are up early and are on the trek by 7.30am. We walk through some beautiful valleys on the way and along the frozen river for a while before crossing it and starting the climb to nearly 5000m at our penultimate stop before Everest Base Camp. I can feel the excitement building that I am getting closer, and remind myself that it will be worth the struggle I am feeling. The final gentle climb to Loboche is a welcome relief compared to some of the steep climbs today, and I am grateful for this as I am really struggling with the altitude.

> "Set a goal to achieve something that is so big, so exhilarating that it excites you and scares you at the same time. It must be a goal that is so appealing, so much in line with your spiritual core that you can't get it out of your mind. If you do not get chills when you set a goal, you're not setting big enough goals"
> Bob Proctor

It takes us over seven grueling hours to get there and I am noticing the increasing symptoms that are taking over my body. I am sticking with my mantra 'One foot in front of the other, up, up, up. It's all about the climb' and it really helps! The headaches and palpitations have been mainly noticeable at night up until now, but they are part of my journey too, along with a tingling sensation in my upper body.

I feel like I have 'pins and needles', and an increasing feeling of light-headedness that is becoming quite worrying, and I begin to doubt my resolve. I have admitted that I have AMS to myself I think and I hope that it remains manageable. The experiences of Dingboche have taken their toll and I find the need to constantly bolster my mental state. I tell myself I can do this – and try my best mind over matter.

Lunch is a huge struggle for me. Another orange menu, another bowl of noodle soup! The liquid I can manage, but the noodles have to be forced down one bite at a time, and they seem to taste of nothing! Bland and yet horrible at the same time – I can't really explain it, but my body doesn't want them! I tell myself that I need the energy for tomorrows climb, but it does little to take the edge off. There is nothing like that feeling of utter dread when you are presented with another orange laminated menu to order a meal, when you know exactly what it contains already and that there is nothing that you want to eat on it. Not only that, but you know that the quality of the food will probably give you food poisoning – that's when you really lose your appetite! Add to that the AMS symptoms of general loss of appetite and trekking for seven hours a day becomes a bit of a challenge!

To make things worse I notice that I have become the centre of attention for a couple of trekkers from a different group. I finally finish after about 30 minutes and my spectators, an Israeli fellow and his girlfriend approach me to tell me that they think I have the mountain sickness and that I must go back down to the next village – 300m below us. Now I have just taken three hours to get here from there on my last trek, and have no desire to undo my hard work! So I thank him for his concern and go back to my new freezing room.

It is not long before I am approached by my guide who the Israeli has also had a word with to express his concerns. Damber is worried for me, despite our fairly frank conversations over my health since I first felt ill at Namche. This is understandable, as the guides are told that if one of their group dies in their care whilst trekking that they will be taken to Britain to be tried for murder.

> "Believe and act as if it were impossible to fail"
> Charles F. Kettering

The feeling of panic in me now is greater than all of my symptoms. I suddenly realise the possibility that I may not do this – and I am only one day away from Everest. There is no way that I want to fail this challenge – but the stories of fatalities on the mountains are running round my head. I tell myself that I feel okay and that I can do this – I can manage to keep going. I have done the training, and I have been managing the sickness up until now. It feels unfair for someone to interfere with my journey. On the other hand, I know that it is the people who push themselves, against the advice, that are the ones who collapse and die on the mountain. I had seen the memorials earlier today just after our first tea break.

After a huge climb of around an hour we had been stunned by the sheer volume of memorials at the top of the trek where literally hundreds of trekkers and mountaineers were remembered by large mounds of rocks and tribute messages. One of them was a woman who had died on the return from Base Camp just last summer.

With these thoughts milling round my head I was in a quandary and thankfully Aimi popped in to see me and we discussed the possibility of starting some of the drugs available for the altitude problems. Damber was recommending them at this point – but it was a huge deal, and I knew there were some side effects. With the agreement of the group I decide to take the Diamax and carry on tomorrow. I so want to do this, I am so close now.

NLP Tips for controlling the inner dialogue

- Turn the volume down

- Look up and gain a new positive perspective

- Turn the voice into a cartoon character

- Turn up the speed of the voice – like a chipmunk

- Turn down the speed of the voice – so it becomes deep and ridiculous

It is vital to control the inner voice that attempts to sabotage your dreams – so deal with it!

I make it up to 5000m on our hike, and I feel better for it. The inspiring views of the edge of Base Camp lift my spirits tremendously. My main obstacle now is to try to avoid my helpful friend at the evening meal, so that I can stay on the mountain. I will do this, and I will survive to tell the tale – well write the book anyhow!

> ### Extract from the 'Bisco Blog'
>
> **Aimi writes:** The morning's walk was steady and the landscape became more and more barren. Not only was plant life now lacking, but there were less and less birds in the sky too. This was an odd reminder that the climate up here is not supposed to sustain life. The sight and sound of rescue helicopters was a constant reminder of those not reaching their destination so, once again, we dug deep to maintain our motivation and arrived at Thukla for a well-earned cup of tea.
>
> At the end of our ascent we reached a profound memorial to those who have climbed in the Everest region and have fallen. An overwhelmingly humbling experience and a stark reminder of the sheer awesomeness of nature. The stories of those who had achieved the summit many times before falling were, perhaps, the most troubling of all. Proof that these mountains can beat even the most experienced climbers. The final ascent was steady and we reached Lobuche by lunchtime. A quick meal of chapati and honey and we were climbing again, to just over 5000m. Here was the greatest reward of all: a sighting of the Khumbu Glacier and the very edge of Base Camp. Suddenly, it all became possible…Tomorrow we walk to Everest Base Camp.

I finally sit down and list my symptoms so far, I have been avoiding admitting any of this to myself let alone anyone else – in my conversations with Damber I have been playing them down:

- Headaches, particularly at night and it has led to loss of sleep
- Nausea
- Palpitations
- Seeing stars/blinding lights in the middle of the night
- 'Pins and needles'
- Stomach ache
- Extreme loss of appetite
- Loose bowels

I ponder on my list and wonder what tomorrow will bring. Our evening discussion with Damber doesn't help – we will be leaving at 5.00am tomorrow for another six hour trek. But it is to Everest – I think that will inspire me to keep going!

Visualisation

There were various times during my Everest experience that visualisation was extremely helpful. This is where you start to picture various events and the successful outcomes that you want. It can be a powerful motivator – and that is how it worked for me.

During my training for the trek there were times when I found it extremely hard – more so when it became disconnected from my longer term goal of Everest. It was at times like this that I would start to imagine climbing towards Everest, and picturing what the experience would be like. In this sense I could connect what I was doing with my big goal and imagine the success I would have because of the work I was currently putting in. In this sense it linked me to my purpose.

Ironically, when on the mountain and starting to find things difficult, I would picture being back in training, on familiar territory – and suddenly the actual climb didn't seem so daunting, it was just another trek on the training trail. Visualisation is an incredibly powerful and useful tool to have in your armoury – and I can testify to its effectiveness.

Trek Six: The Trek to Everest Base Camp.

It is barely 4.30am. Eating breakfast this early is my first challenge of the day, and as I watch the girls struggle with their porridge, I am glad to have opted for toast and jam this morning. It doesn't help however; my body still doesn't want the food. I find this constant battle between my mind and my mouth at every meal. My mind is trying to tell me that I need the food for energy – my mouth, in conjunction with my stomach, is merely working on the gag reflex! But I eat, finish (do I actually punch the air in celebration?) and we are on our way. It is rocky and a mix of up and down as we climb to around 5200m at Gorakshep where we stop for a second breakfast (yes we all feel like Hobbits!) another piece of toast for me that I struggle to get inside.

> "Goals provide the energy source that powers our lives. One of the best ways we can get the most from the energy we have is to focus it. That is what goals can do for us; concentrate our energy"
> Denis Waitley

Soon we are off on the final leg – the last three hour trek to Everest Base Camp. I am happily ignoring all of my symptoms today; I can feel the excitement building as I work towards the final part of my goal. When we stop to view Everest, I am awed that I am actually here. I am looking at the 'top of the world' with my own eyes, and I am desperate for a photo at the closest point to the beast of a mountain. Of course, you can't see the actual mountain from Base Camp, and so this is the best it gets until I climb to the summit! We get a mini-boost as we come across a sign for 'Everest this way', and a pose for photos is essential; one for the Facebook page perhaps? One of many maybe!

When we pause for a water break we take in the view of the original Base Camp that Sir Edmund Hillary established – and I ponder that he would have been there exactly 60 years ago. I find this strangely inspiring, and it dwarfs my achievements somewhat – I am so crippled with altitude sickness that the thought of another 3000m is somewhat debilitating! However, I will ignore all of that when I tell the tale of my goal achievement at EBC when I get home!

Three hours trekking and we are finally at Everest Base Camp 5350m. It is time to celebrate, have some more photos, and Ellie is kind enough to share her phone as I speak to Emma and Lisa from Everest! It is with emotion and exhilaration when I hear Emma's 'Wow' when I tell her where I am calling from. One of those special moments that makes all of this worthwhile. After about half an hour we are on our way back to Gorakshep – and find the time to reflect on the achievements of the day!

I write in my diary 'I made Base Camp today. Seven days of solid walking pretty much and I have achieved my goal! It is probably the hardest thing I have ever done – even than the London Marathon, which was tough! I have overcome illness as well as dealing with the physical strain on my body. It has been unbelievable and I have had to literally will each step at times. I have proved that I can climb any mountain – one step at a time. I have shown myself that I have incredible determination and resolve when I need it. Once I have committed to a goal I will achieve it, no matter what – what else do I need to start applying this to?'

"The truth of the matter is that there's nothing you can't accomplish if: (1) You clearly decide what it is that you're absolutely committed to achieving, (2) You're willing to take massive action, (3) You notice what's working or not, and (4) You continue to change your approach until you achieve what you want, using whatever life gives you along the way"
Anthony Robbins

I also have a little reflection on my phone call 'So lovely to speak to my family today – thank you Ellie – hearing Emma and Lisa's voices was fabulous and reminded me I am connected somewhere in this bleak and beautiful place when I feel so estranged. I didn't know how much I would miss them and I have shocked myself. Now each step is a step towards home and family!'

Extract from the 'Bisco Blog'

Aimi writes: As we edged around the final boulder, we saw the sign; we were there. It was impossible to tell if the welled eyes were relief it was done, or thrill at the achievement. Though reaching the destination was utter fulfillment, we had already realised that the adventure had been in the journey. A bizarre satellite signal afforded much needed, albeit brief, phone calls home. We celebrated with rum and biscuits before preparing ourselves for the long walk home. The walk back to Gorakshep was swifter, past the site of Hillary's original Base Camp and back to our tea house with its treacherous, frozen toilet floor.

Trek Seven: The Beginning of the End…Return to Orsho

> 'Energy is the persistence to conquer all things'
> Benjamin Franklin
>
> "The basic goal-reaching principle is to understand that you go as far as you can see, and when you get there you will always be able to see farther"
> Zig Ziglar

I guess you could call it a disturbed night's sleep. I awoke several times regretting the egg fried rice I had for tea last evening. It was that sometimes familiar feeling following too much Chinese – only in my case it was a third of a plate! By 4.30am I was up to get ready for the climb to the summit of Kala Patthar, but my tummy had other plans!

I suppose you can't call it 'Delhi belly' when you are in the north of Nepal, a few miles from the border of Tibet – but the feeling is the same! So whilst the girls encountered the most difficult climb of their lives, I was assaulting the squat toilet with my liquid belly! By the time the girls had finished their climb, eaten breakfast and got packed to leave – I had managed five visits to the iced up loo, and was feeling a little worse for wear! Check out Aimi's blog for the amazing time that the girls had whilst I evacuated everything!

What followed was a day of endurance like I had never faced before, as we trekked for two hours at a time across the valleys we had travelled up a few days earlier – only this time we were going double speed to cover two days of trekking in one. By the time we left from lunch my stomach was finally done – the second Imodium seemed to take care of that.

> "Goals are not only absolutely necessary to motivate us. They are essential to really keep us alive"
> Robert H. Schiller

It was a day of mind over matter, as I trekked with very little energy and the elation of reaching EBC the day before seemed to disappear in pure concentration! One step after another, I knew I could do this – but there was little left over to take in the amazing views around me. The girls jubilation over their triumph of Kala Patthar did little to lift my spirits, as I realised I had missed out on something special – I had to console myself with the thought that it was not on my goal list, and therefore not part of my agenda for this trip.

NLP Presuppositions that supported me on the Everest Trail

'If it is possible for one person, then it is possible for me'

'I have all the resources I need'

'There is no failure only feedback – I was able to listen to the feedback around me and make adjustments and improvements'

'The mind affects my body – they are part of the same system'

'The most flexible controls the system – I was able to be extremely flexible and adaptable, changing with many new circumstances'

'I am in charge of my mind and therefore my results'

I tried a little dry toast for tea, happy not to have to leave for another acclimatisation hike now that we were on the way down. I had been anticipating feeling so fit for the journey back as we dropped in altitude – but I was still tingling from the thighs up, still getting the headaches, and feeling extremely weary. I manage to stop myself from wondering what this is all for – just! But it was a difficult day for me, and I was glad to lie down for the night.

Extract from the 'Bisco Blog'

Aimi writes: The darkness masked the scene and it was a crunching sound underfoot that gave away the change. Directing head torches to the ground, we could see that a blanket of snow had fallen overnight.
Kala Patthar now stood before us, not as a black rocky mountain, but as a heightened challenge, exacerbated by its coating of snow and ice. We walked tentatively towards it and began to climb, before long realising that we had underestimated the scale of this mountain. Suddenly, this became a trip of two parts. Base Camp had been a feat of endurance, this was something else altogether. When those ahead of you are stopping to vomit or buckle to their knees, you know it's going to take all you have to summit. Though there were moments of doubt, we reached the summit of New Kala Patthar (5700-5800m by D's estimation) ten minutes before the sun rose. Then it became clear why we had just put ourselves through the most physically challenging two hours of our lives: the sun rose directly behind the peak of Mount Everest. Suffice to say, it will be a struggle to find a picture that beautiful again in a lifetime.

Then we began our journey home, with an immediate sighting of some comically rotund Tibetan snow cocks. Though we had a long distance to cover, the descent was like bouncing on clouds as the air thickened with oxygen in each step taken. Lots more yak traffic today, including one rogue beast who almost took Ellie out. We also faced our strongest winds yet as we now walked through, instead of above, the valley. It is important to add at this juncture that all blog posts from here on out will have a distinctly chirpier tone. Ellie thinks it was Buddha who said "You have to reach the depths of despair to truly appreciate pure joy." Regardless of who said it, in the context of the Himalayas, they were right on the money.

Trek Eight: Back to Namche Bazar

> "Nothing limits achievement like small thinking; nothing expands possibilities like unleashed imagination"
> William Arthur Ward

I awoke feeling quite refreshed and after a little toast and jam I was ready for the trek. I started to look forward to showering at Namche – and maybe even a little souvenir shopping!

The day is brightening up as we drop down in altitude, and the warmth of the sun brightens my mood considerably, I write that I am loving the journey to Tengboche. After a couple of hours of climbing we are at the highest monastery in the world – well I suppose it would be up here at 4000m! It is intense up and down as far as the trek goes, but I am starting to feel the benefit of dropping in altitude at last – I even feel slightly fit! I know I can do this – what a difference a day makes, along with some food in the stomach! I remember that I am still here for the climb, and that I can handle the one foot in front of the other. It is still up, up, up but I have endured worse feelings than this. I start to feel like the intrepid explorer that I always wanted to be!

> "An idea that is developed and put into action is more important than an idea that exists only as an idea"
> Buddha

After seven hours trekking we round the final corner into the hill town of Namche – and it strangely feels like civilisation and home! After a shower and a change of clothes I venture out and manage to find the first of my souvenir presents for Emma – some local jewellery and small carved boxes. I am actually starting to feel well again – the first time since I left here seven days ago, and I can begin to take stock of what I have achieved. It feels great – I want to remember this feeling – perhaps I should write the book after all!

Extract from the 'Bisco Blog'

Aimi writes: The walk to Tengboche was a little slower than we'd hoped as we found ourselves stuck behind the slowest herd of dzopjke (yak-cows) we had yet encountered. If anything, it gave us an excuse to take the big uphill push at a leisurely pace and, by mid-morning, we had reached the quiet heights of Tengboche.

We took a few moments to visit the beautiful (and world's highest) monastery. The building was exquisite and radiating with colour. It then seemed something of a paradox to walk outside to a swarm of armed Nepalese soldiers. Suffice to say, we made a quick exit and continued our journey to Kanjuna for our lunch stop. There were a surprising number of uphill slogs and, having lost almost 2000m in two days, we were back in the thick heat. After an age of walking, we descended the stony steps to Namche Bazaar.

Inevitably, we found ourselves pinned to a very dusty wall as a herd of two dozen fully-laden donkeys came charging up the path. Ears, tails and dust were flying in all directions and, when we thought they had passed, there came the familiar sound of yak bells from above. There was a brief moment of freedom between the herds where Aimi and our porter decided to make a break for it, leaping into a side alley just before the herd came thundering past. After that excitement, we went straight to the tea house for our first shower in a week. This may seem unpleasant, but D has just revealed it was his first shower in two months…Tomorrow is our final day of trekking. Tonight we celebrate!

Trek Nine: Lukla again...

> "Enthusiasm is one of the most powerful engines of success. When you do a thing, do it with all your mind. Put your whole soul to it. Stamp it with your own personality. Be active, be energetic, be enthusiastic and faithful, and you will accomplish your object. Nothing great was ever achieved without enthusiasm"
> Ralph Waldo Emerson

I am reminded of the simplicity of life here as I am awoken by the sound of a cockerel crowing as he marches up and down the main street in Namche. Somehow it makes me smile, and I remember that I am the visitor here, and feel privileged to be a part of this small community if only for a short time longer. By lunch time we are back in Phakding, having circumnavigated the bridges once more – and going down the hardest trek is so much easier than ascending as I had done a just over a week ago.

On the journey there is plenty of time to gather a few memories on my phone which is now charged up, and I am snapping my final views of the territory. It was with some sadness that I took my final snap of Everest yesterday, and today it is all about the river valley and being surrounded by the huge mountains I had recently been aloft! This is a stunning part of the world, and to be highly recommended to any would be tourist/adventurer.

> "Big goals get big results. No goal gets no results or somebody else's results"
> Mark Victor Hansen

Now that I am feeling well and fit again, I have time and headspace to begin to reflect on what this trip of a lifetime has given me. I know I am changed, but it is difficult to put it into words. I do know that it is all good – and somehow I have experienced something that will start to put my whole life into perspective. I ask myself the question 'What have you lost in your life that you want to take back?' I will let that sit awhile as I ponder on the silence of the trail.

By mid-afternoon we are back in Lukla, and I walk through the gateway to the Sagarmathar National Park – and know that I have achieved something special. I had no idea how difficult this trek would be, and my little walk in the mountains has taught me so much about how I handle the difficult times. I have endured and I have survived, and somehow have conquered many of my demons. What a great feeling!

A couple of hours later I am sat in Starbucks in Lukla (yes I know!! Aimi was disgusted; I was over the moon!!), and it is amazing what you appreciate after it's been given back! I am loving my first vanilla latte in over two weeks, plus I nearly cried when I saw my room in the tea house at Lukla – it actually has an ensuite bathroom with a *flushing* loo!! Right now I could actually live here!

> "The more intensely we feel about an idea or a goal, the more assuredly the idea, buried deep in our subconscious, will direct us along the path to its fulfillment"
> Earl Nightingale

To be back in Lukla is something of a landmark, as you can imagine. The ten day trek is over, and I am struck with a huge sense of achievement. It has truly been the hardest challenge of my life to date. To achieve the full trek in only ten days was incredible. It was twelve days originally which we had already condensed to eleven, and then finally finished in ten as we lost two acclimatisation days from the journey. It was done in the most difficult of circumstances, and for me was an incredible achievement – when you take into account my list of AMS symptoms and the food poisoning at Gorakshep.

I have lost two notches on my belt which I guess stands to reason as I have been walking around seven hours a day whilst eating next to nothing – and some days literally nothing! I don't know how I found the energy – but I did!

Digging deep into my reserves I have pushed myself beyond my previous limits. I have faced and conquered fears – heights, bridges, and of course squat toilets! I have found new strengths and extended my comfort zone. I know I can achieve what I put all my energy into. I am a completer-finisher. I *can* do endurance. I have achieved so much more than in my marathon running – and I am proud of all those too!

The Size of your Thinking

When it came to my dream for Everest – it was about thinking big. In fact it was about thinking beyond what I thought was possible. Thinking small limits you, but there s a 'magic' about thinking big. Somehow it unlocks the resourceful you – as you search for solutions to make your big dream happen. It is about going for more, looking to expand your circle as you move out of your comfort zone. One of the mantras for our trip was a diagram that Aimi came across – and now appears on our souvenir 'hoody' sweatshirts. It shows a comfort zone in a circle, and an arrow pointing outside of the circle stating 'Where the good stuff happens'. I like that! It really sums up the trip for me. Sometimes it is just a case of 'behaving as if' you have already succeeded – and the big thinking kicks in to bring it about.

What about you? Are you ready to step out of your comfort zone into the place where the 'good stuff' could happen for you? What is stopping you? Start making plans!

I am able to reflect on how all of my training actually did prepare me for this. It actually started last summer in Majorca as I chose to ascend over 500 steps every few days in amongst my running, which has stood me in good stead for the endless stairs of the up and down on the valley sides. I was up early in the morning to 'Beat the Bore' running over seven miles before breakfast alongside the river Severn – to get me in the mind-set of leaving early every morning on the trail. The uphill slog over trails of the Tough Ten and the sides of Cribyn and Pen y Fan all have made me ready for the endless uphill trails of the Everest trek. When I have felt shattered and unfit – I remember that I trained hard for this, but it remained the most difficult journey of my life. I am so glad that I did it – no-one can take that from me!

The question is: 'What is next for me? What do I really want to do with my life?' What about for you? Will you take your 'mountain'? What is it for you?

Extract from the 'Bisco Blog'

Aimi writes: It was difficult to know whether to will for the end of the trek to arrive, or wish it never to end. Either way, we walked on very tired legs and feet that were now wholeheartedly rejecting the suffocation of walking boots. It was a strange feeling to pass trekkers setting out on their first day of walking. Most had little to say but just smiled and stared with a look of "have you really achieved it?" in their eyes. It is a sentiment which resonated with us all from our early days of walking, so we were just able to smile and nod, harbouring the simple thought of "Yes. Yes I have."

Communities grew more populated as we walked and a beautiful little boy came charging up to offer a sprig of berries just as we approached Lukla. We will never forget how incredibly welcome we have been made to feel. The final ascent into Lukla was a push, but we paced into the town with high-fives all round. Tonight we eat, rest, say a fond farewell to our lovely porters and keep everything crossed for clear skies tomorrow to ease our return to Kathmandu.

Kathmandu again...

> "Your purpose explains what you are doing with your life. Your vision explains how you are living your purpose. Your goals enable you to realize your vision"
> Bob Proctor

The flight back from Lukla was another exciting encounter with the short runway and the airwaves. Having survived the chaos of the check-in and 'security' procedures that somehow works beautifully despite appearances, I sat waiting for the plane.

I watch with trepidation as our guide leaves happily ahead of us on the first flight, leaving us to hope the second flight would fly today. Nevertheless, I am soon airborne again and looking forward to the relative civilisation in the strange sprawling anarchy of the Kathmandu highways. Again I am amazed as this shouldn't work – nobody, therefore everybody gives way – and yet the traffic weaves slowly with a terrifying fluidity. The sounds of car horns punctuate the journey from beginning to end – it is quite the experience!

The early morning flight from Lukla guaranteed that we arrived safely back in Kathmandu by breakfast time, and so here I am back in the Kathmandu Guest House – the 'trekking central' of Nepal. It feels quite surreal to be back. Kathmandu is such an enigmatic city – and it is strange to call it civilisation, but that is what it is compared to where I have been in the small villages of the Himalayas. Yet here I am in a developing city where poverty and affluence sit uncomfortably side by side.

Out for breakfast I struggle to fit in the cooked food, as my appetite has shrunk so much, but I am starting to feel human again. A hint that my appetite will return soon enough I'm sure. In Kathmandu - shopping and circumnavigating the traffic and the traders proves exhausting. There literally are no rules here! Everyone is looking for something from you. The bartering is intense. The traffic relentless. It is a hard place, a desperate place with so many looking to get out. It really is culture shock in so many ways.

Following in the footsteps of others

Modelling is one of the foundations of NLP. I call it standing on the shoulders of giants, and it is based on the NLP presupposition that 'if one person can, then anyone can'. I was so excited to see the original Base Camp on the way to the current location, and I started to picture Hillary and his team sixty years ago getting ready for the assent in May 1953.

However, the inspiration for trekking to Base Camp was not an effort to model Hilary's strategy, but was based on the simple success principle of one of my heroes – Miles Hilton-Barber. He is a blind adventurer that I met a few years ago. After listening to him I came to realise that people are just people – and all are only human. Therefore, if they can achieve – then so can I. Miles' strategy is simple: Dream, decide, plan and persevere. I can handle that!

Modelling for me was about drawing on Miles as a person. If a blind person such as him can have such great adventures – then so can I. I have no excuse not to do something with my life. I started to believe that I could follow in his footsteps – by just making a plan and then doing it. I found myself taking on his values and beliefs as I started to plan my adventures. I still believe that this is just one of many to come. I am only limited by my imagination.

Modelling is more to do with hard work and the determination to acquire the necessary skills than it is to do with raw talent – as most athletes will attest to. It is just a case of starting and then experimenting until you get it right – and being prepared to put the work in as you grow.

What about you? Who are your models? What are you going to dream for? When will you start to make your plans?

The irony is that we from the West come looking for a sense of awe and inner peace in this part of the world. They are looking for a way out. In times of economic hardship that we are facing – they are looking to us; desperate to leave for a better life. Damber talked of his broken dreams of getting out through the British Ghurkas when he damaged his hand in a farming accident. Now he can only talk of the rest of his family who have achieved this and live in Reading. For him, Britain still represents the dream. It makes me want to appreciate what I have a new way, I suppose.

Peace in the mountains?

What about me: Did I find peace in the mountains? Maybe... I certainly think I was awed around every turn. Interestingly, when I was higher up, the going was so tough that I could rarely look up and see the beauty of the mountains. It became about survival and mind over matter.

> "Take up one idea. Make that one idea your life - think of it, dream of it, and live on that idea. Let the brain, muscles, nerves, every part of your body, be full of that idea, and just leave every other idea alone. This is the way to success"
> Swami Vivekananda

I think you need time to find peace in the mountains which I rarely had. Maybe now that I have two days in Kathmandu, with free time on my hands, I can find the peace of the mountains amongst the chaos of the fast-sell bartering culture.

I write in my diary 'The beauty of the mountains will stay with me, I still feel privileged to have seen perhaps the greatest mountains this world has to offer. Certainly they are the highest, and all so incredibly impressive, alongside the constant of the river. The sound of rushing water amongst the rocks, below beautiful mountains, is my favourite sound of the trek – I have always managed to 'lose myself' in the sound of rushing water.'

> "A dream is just a dream. A goal is a dream with a plan and a deadline"
> Harvey Mackay

At the KGH it is lovely to discover emails from Emma and Lisa, I am feeling much less estranged as Saturday – and home – looms before me. It is good to take some time to appreciate what I am missing of home, and to allow myself the luxury of contemplating a reunion. Tomorrow I visit the project that we have raised money for through our sponsorship for doing this amazing challenge. Anticipation in me is quite high, to say the least. Perhaps it will put my own challenges to scale the heights to Everest Base Camp into perspective...let's see what tomorrow will bring.

Extract from the 'Bisco Blog'

Aimi writes: Back in Kathmandu, we felt a home away from home. We ate a continental breakfast, showered and found the indulgent relief of stowed clean clothes. A day was spent shopping and in a blur of disbelief as to the extent of the previous fortnight's adventure. There was time to access the internet, confirm our safe arrival to loved ones and then reward the enormous contribution of our stupendous guide D with a well earned feast and a bottle of locally brewed ale.

The evening was a chance to reflect on achievements and celebrate what had passed. We were united as a team and bound as individuals through shared experience. Not too late to bed as tomorrow we visit the FfN project schools to cement to purpose of this inexplicable ordeal.

Future for Nepal...

> "When we seek to discover the best in others, we somehow bring out the best in ourselves"
> William Arthur Ward

What an intriguing day. We are picked up soon after breakfast by Prerana from FfN, and whisked across Kathmandu and on through the outlying villages to visit one of their project schools where we are shown incredible hospitality and also the library that they have supplied through FfN funding. It will be something like this that our money will be used for. The next stop is the private school that started the ball rolling for FfN when founder Tom visited here on a placement eight years ago as a volunteer. It is now the school where their sponsored pupils from the surrounding villages are sent for their private education.

I write in my diary 'No answers today, just a lot of questions on my mind. I have met with the charity we are fundraising for – Future for Nepal – and visited some of their projects. This involved a trip out of Kathmandu into the surrounding villages in the valley to see one of their schools, and then a look at a school in the inner city metropolis of Kathmandu itself. I have heard much about how the passion of a young man eight years ago has led to some amazing and effective targeted work amongst some of the young people of Nepal. It is truly inspiring to see what can be achieved in a short space of time when you have a passionate vision for something that you believe in. It begs the question: 'What is it for me?'

If I can broaden it out into a coaching agenda 'What is it for you?' What do you need to take back? What 'mountain' do you need to take? Do you want to make a real difference somewhere? What is it that you are passionate about? Enough to do something...?

I feel inspired, challenged, amazed – so what will I do about it when I get home? I thought that I had done it – completed my challenge on the trek to EBC – but perhaps I haven't even started yet...

The passion and heart of these people is astounding, and it was so lovely today to meet some of the pupils who have been sponsored to go to school by FfN, and some of their teachers. To see the hunger for education and improvement was fabulous. It reminded me of my conversation with Damber who expressed such a desperate desire – on behalf of all his people – to get on in life somehow.

I write in my diary 'I am particularly moved by the effectiveness of Tom and Prerana at FfN. The vision to transform the villages around Kathmandu one young person at a time is quite incredible. It is so simple, yet so powerful. One child is sponsored to get an education then sent back to help develop their village. As a teacher I have always believed in the power of education to transform lives – but this is something else! It is fabulous to see how education is valued as the power to transform the villages from poverty to survival and beyond. The way we were treated like royalty and such special visitors was humbling in itself. What a privilege to be introduced to these fabulous people!'

Extract from the 'Bisco Blog'

Aimi writes: Prerana turned out to be one of the kindest and most driven people we had ever met. Most importantly of all, she is an inspiring realist. The day was not designed to tug heart strings with tales of woe and suffering. It was not a day deserving of sadness or a contrived, melancholic soundtrack. Today was about two very simple things: inspiration and hope. We drove out of the city into the villages and arrived at a beautiful little school. We were draped in khatas (ceremonial scarves) and treated like royalty when discovered to be teachers ourselves. The principal was an exceptional man, stretching tiny allocations of money to provide the very best English-medium education possible for his 550 students. With a few books, lab beakers and some very dated computers, he was educating and inspiring a generation of young people to strive for excellence.

That was the moment we realised. FfN is not about dramatic rescues. FfN simply allows children to learn, shielding them from the chaos of a country with no real government or constitution for a few hours a day so that they can have a fighting chance of survival and success. The next school we visited just fixed this reality for us. A handful of sponsored children brought into boarding school; a ten year commitment to change the lives of real, individual children. Most importantly, respect is demanded for family and culture. Every holiday these children return to their families and enrich their communities. FfN does not assume to make 'new lives' for children, its work allows them to live the lives they have. Seems so simple doesn't it?

Future for Nepal believes passionately that education is the key for changing the future for these people, and it was humbling to be held in such high regard as teachers here. They literally treated us like royalty. The vision of FfN to improve these children's lives, improve their chances through better facilities, and then sending them back into their communities as ambassadors for change is striking in its simple genius. The communities are literally changing one life at a time on a cycle of improvement.

I am also struck by the kindness of Prerana to us personally who wanted to treat us like tourists for the day and showed us the best parts of the city of Kathmandu and took us to lunch in a lovely restaurant. She then invited us up to the share in their family time of reflection for a dead friend at the 'Monkey Temple' overlooking the city and indeed the whole of the Kathmandu valley. She and her husband were happy to play tourist guides for us, and proved a mine of information.

Values rediscovered on the Everest Trail

Do you know what is important to you? In NLP we talk of values and beliefs – the things that are vitally important to you, and the beliefs to support them. This will affect the choices you make with your life – are they positive choices that you are in charge of and in line with your values, or are you being pushed around by intrinsic inherited beliefs that are controlling your choices in a negative way? If you are not careful while you are busy the important things and people can get lost.

NLP is about making positive choices for your life in line with what is really important to you. Are you feeling uncomfortable with certain areas of your life? These are signals that you are not living in line with your values and what is really important to you.

Take some time to face your values, take the discovery test:
Think back to a time that you felt uncomfortable with an area of your life.

- Ask yourself 'What is important to me about.....' fill in the area of discomfort. Follow up with the question 'What else is important to me about....' and continue to ask yourself until you have a full list. List the values you have uncovered about yourself.
- Ask yourself 'Which of these is the most important to me?' in order to gain a sense of priority in your values.
- Now consider: Are you living in line with your values? Where you are living out of line with your values you need to start to consider the choices you are making with your life. Will you?

For me, the main challenge to my life from the mountain was in this area. I noticed that I had rediscovered some of my values from my earlier life that I wanted to reclaim. I think that is what has made the biggest difference to me, and the most lasting change. I really value these people, choices, lifestyle and I want to make them a priority in the future. What will you do when you discover you are living contrary to your values? Will you make some changes today?

Values help align you with your overall purpose, and I realise that my experience on the mountain showed me where I had become misaligned and my reflections have allowed me to start to realign my life once again. This is about being clear on the desired outcomes – I was able to see what I really wanted for my life. What about you? Do you know what your desired results are? What outcomes do you want from your life?

The Return

> "If you believe you can, you probably can. If you believe you won't, you most assuredly won't. Belief is the ignition switch that gets you off the launching pad"
> Denis Waitley

I am leaving Kathmandu today with mixed emotions. I am desperate to get back to my family and some sense of normality (whatever that is!), but I shall miss Nepal. I have had such an amazing collection of experiences that a part of me wants to hold on to them a little longer.

The memories are already fading and in some ways it is hard to imagine it was me going through the challenge of a lifetime. A couple of days in the chaos of Thamel, Kathmandu and the feelings of calm and tranquility of the mountains are gone. I guess the real trick is to take the place with you when you go. One thing I know, I leave a different person to when I came having discovered a new determination for my life. I have also rediscovered some forgotten priorities for my life. It has truly been life changing I suppose.

As I look out of the airplane window I have one last glance at the Himalayas and head for Delhi, and then on to Heathrow and the rest of my life...

Everest – The Mountain analogy

The mountain peak has long been a symbol of success and the idea of climbing mountains associated with achievement. At the top of the mountain the view is clear and unobstructed, it is inspiring and there is a feeling of being 'on top of things'. From the mountain top you are able to look further and gain a new perspective on things. My experience at Everest gave me all of this and more at various times during my trek. It was a truly inspiring time, and a time for thoughtful reflection as I gained a new perspective and enjoyed the satisfaction of achievement.

NLP is full of references to your 'peak state' and the idea of peak performance. Here, the literal mountain peak becomes an analogy for the successful state you can access through NLP. Your characteristics when in your peak state include:

- You are committed to a mission larger than you
- You are purposeful
- You measure your results
- You are a great team player
- You are able to make corrections and adjustments
- You are flexible
- You are able to maintain momentum
- You can change with the times
- You have a strong belief in your success
- You believe you can make a difference
- You are highly motivated
- You desire to be at the top of your performance

I recognise so many of these things as being part of the success of my Everest experience – I learned so much about digging deeper into my resources so that I could succeed in my mission and purpose. What about you? What is your mission? Have you realised your purpose? Where do you want to make a difference? Will you start to access your peak state to achieve what you want?

Managing your state

An essential part of achieving your peak state is the ability to manage your state, eliminating the negative states to make room for the peak. Good management of your state of mind and emotions is about knowing yourself. It is about recognising a slip negativity and making adjustments to put you back into a more positive and resourceful state. NLP calls this calibration – making fine adjustments.

You must know when you are feeling positive, and know how to put yourself into this positive state. What are your triggers for negativity? What are your positive triggers?

- Recognise your state

- Change your state by making adjustments – do something different

- Release your inner resources and positivity to find your peak state

- Enjoy your peak state

PART THREE: THE AFTERMATH

REFLECTIONS ON MY TRIP

What next?

A week on and I how do I feel about my Everest trek?

As the trek starts to become a bit of a blur in the mix of school, rehearsals and paperwork I realise that I have been changed by the experience at Everest Base Camp. I do feel different. I know deep down that I have achieved something quite special.

It was so hard at times, and I have to remind myself of that as the memory fades. It was hard but I achieved it! I want to keep that alive for myself. If I can do that I know there is so much more I can achieve in my life. I can climb any mountain – one step at a time. Sometimes it is as simple as putting one foot in front of the other and keeping going regardless of how it feels.

> "If you want to live a happy life, tie it to a goal, not to people or things"
> Albert Einstein

Of course, there is the part of me that is subconsciously planning my next adventure. In fact the question is I've been asked the most is: 'Would you do it again?' And I always reply that there is so much to do and see in this world I'm not sure I would repeat the adventure to Everest for the sake of it. In fact if I do return it will be to make the summit! But what will I do next? Maybe Mount Kilimanjaro in Africa, maybe a visit to the North Pole? I also want to travel to South America too. There is so much that I want to achieve, so many places that I would like to go adventuring, and I don't want to limit myself in any way. That is how changed I feel – it literally changes everything.

I also feel changed because of the brush with Developing World poverty, and I feel strangely humbled and grateful for the life I have been given. There is more to do here and I am considering carefully what I have been put here to do. What is my purpose regarding affecting the world and bringing about a change somewhere. I have been inspired by the work of Tom at FfN, and how simply and effectively they are making a difference to a few children. All are making a difference to their communities one life at a time. What is it for me? What one thing is my priority to bring about positive change in the world?

Post script: Reflections from the Wenallt - again!

> "Create a definite plan for carrying out your desire, and begin at once, whether you're ready or not, to put it into action"
> Napoleon Hill

So I am back up the Wenallt after four weeks of frenetic frenzy at school, and it is time to reflect from a distance my time on the trail. It is a beautiful sunny day – such a contrast to last time on Boxing Day – on a lovely Bank Holiday Weekend. The last time I sat in the sun I was in Nepal. This is the first chance I have had to properly reflect after such a manic month in school.

I loved my time away and have definitely come back a different person somehow – although this is hard to quantify. I think my adventures and just trying out new circumstances have affected me deeply. A glimpse of the poverty of Nepal, as with any developing country, is always humbling, challenging and brings questions over the purpose of life in the West. As before, the view is obscured from the top of the hill – where it used to be so clear – but I know there is something out there. Just like my life – I can't see all of the detail right now, but I know there is something special out there for me.

I think achieving my goal, despite the incredible hardships and challenges on the way, has made the biggest difference to me. I know I have a greater depth of determination than I ever imagined and that I am stronger for it. The idea that I can climb any mountain one step at a time lives on in me – and this has been a sure way of getting through the busyness that is my life in school.

During the last four weeks I have had four projects on the go at once – each of which involve rehearsing the students to performance, and driving the process into perfection for the audience and the examiners. I have found myself literally working through my mantra – one step at a time, just keep going! I can climb even this kind of mountain, and it has helped me through as I dig into my reserves. I didn't exactly start the term on full energy!

Alongside this it has been a term, once again, of knocks from above as I try to adjust to the new management ideas and routines, and my faculty is slashed to pieces in budget cuts. I am learning to keep my chin up, and borrowing my mind over matter mind-set from the mountains. I think this is where the test of my changes really count. How will I continue to draw on my new outlook? I guess one step at a time...

> "Learn to enjoy every minute of your life. Be happy now. Don't wait for something outside of yourself to make you happy in the future. Think how really precious is the time you have to spend, whether it's at work or with your family"
> Earl Nightingale

There is also a sense of a change in priorities – I value my life more in the sense that career isn't as important to me as it had become in recent years. I've rediscovered something of who I was, and gained a new sense of who I want to be. I need to embrace this completely – yet things are already changing. I want to spend more time outside, and I with my family too – preferably both at the same time. I spent most of my childhood outside, ups this 'mountain' in fact, and I have rediscovered a love for the outdoors. I want more adventures and in the meantime I have the constant challenges of running races. This morning was the Bristol 10k and I took a whole five minutes off my PB – which I am more than a little pleased about! I have also entered the ballot for the London 2014 Marathon as it is back in the Easter holidays again!

I have loved my adventure – taking my mountain, and taking back things that I had lost. I really feel different, and that I will continue to 'Take Back my Mountains' for the rest of my life. I am grateful for the experience of a lifetime – so far! I want my life to count – I think I have always needed this sense of purpose, but it so easily gets lost from view.

What's next? For me, I don't know yet – but I am ready for the challenge whatever it may be. What about you? Are you ready to Take Back your Mountain?

THE CHALLENGE

My challenge to you:
- Write a list of three new things to do this year
- Go and do them – make plans today
- Re-take this challenge every year – and watch your life grow into the adventure you always wanted it to be…

"Only those who risk going too far will find out how far it is possible to go"
T. Elliott

"Think left and think right and think low and think high. Oh, the things you can think up if only you try!"
Dr. Seuss

"The important thing is not being afraid to take a chance. Remember, the greatest failure is to not try. Once you find something you love to do, be the best at doing it"
Debbi Fields

GLOSSARY OF TERMS

Accountability: A key part of coaching. You are accountable for your own actions and the progress you make during coaching.

Anchor: A trigger that links with an action or an emotional state for you. Trigger's can be linked to visual, auditory or kinesthetic stimuli.

Beliefs: The generalisations that you hold about your life and your interpretation of the world, that become operating principles. These can be supportive of your life, or may prove limiting to your progress and can be challenged in coaching.

Commitment: An essential part of coaching as you take on a task without question because it is emotionally and cognitively important to the real you.

Congruence: The alignment of beliefs, values, skills and action, so that you are in sync with all areas of your life. It is an agreement or 'unity' between the different parts of a person.

Feedback: The information that you receive as a result of your life experience, positive or negative

Future pacing: Mentally rehearsing or testing an outcome to ensure that your desired behaviour or state will occur.

Goals: Your desired results. Process goals are about your journey, Outcome goals are about your final destination or result.

Identity: Your self-image or self-concept; who you take yourself to be; the totality of your being.

Life balance: The harmony of your relationship with the different parts of your life and its demands.

Neuro-Linguistic Programming: The study of excellence and a model of how individuals structure their experience, created by Richard Bandler and John Grinder in the 1970's.

Map of Reality: Your unique model of the world based on your individual perceptions and experiences.

Outcome: A specific, sensory-based, desired result that meets your criteria.

Presuppositions: Ideas or beliefs that are presupposed and acted upon.

Rapport: A relationship of responsiveness to self or others. Mutual trust and understanding between individuals, facilitating communication.

Reframing: Understanding an experience in a different way, giving it a different meaning. Gaining a different perspective; by changing the frame of reference of a situation or problem.

Representational systems: The different channels whereby you represent information on the inside, using your senses: visual (sight), auditory (hearing), kinesthetic (feelings), olfactory (smell), and gustatory (taste). You may find you have a dominant system.

Resources: Anything that can help you achieve an outcome e.g. states, thoughts, beliefs, strategies, people, possessions, experiences.

State: How you feel, your mood, or state of mind; the sum of all neurological and physical processes within you at any moment.

Strategy: A sequence of representations leading to a particular outcome.

Values: The most important internal criteria that you wish to live by.

Vision: A combination of goals and values, the purpose and greater meaning in life.

Visualisation: The process of seeing images in your mind, sometimes referred to as mental rehearsal.

RECOMMENDED READING

The following is a partial list of the books that I have studied over the last few years as I have trained to become a coach, studied coaching and NLP, and written a dissertation on coaching for my MA! Most of them I have read from cover to cover—as I have become fascinated (some would say obsessed—ask my wife!!) about the amazing potential of coaching to change lives.

I hope you find further inspiration in them as you pursue and excellent life through the world of coaching. In true NLP style I have modelled my book on techniques and ideas from the coaching world and I recommend them to you for your further study.

Adler, H and Heather, B (2003) NLP in 21 Days. Piatkus

Allison, S and Harbour, M. (2009) The Coaching Toolkit. SAGE

Andreas, S and Faulkner, C. (2002) NLP: The New Technology of Achievement. Nicholas Brealey publishing. London

Barber, J (2005) Good Question! The Art of asking questions to bring about positive change. Bookshaker

Bartkowiak, J (2011) Engaging NLP: Teens. MX Publishing: London

Cope, M (2004) The Seven C's of Coaching. Pearson Education Limited. Harlow, England. London.

Downey, M. (2003) Effective Coaching. CENGAGE Learning

Flaherty, J. (1999) Coaching: Evoking excellence in others. London:Butterworth

Gallwey, W. T. (1986) The Inner Game of Tennis. Pan Books

Gallwey, W. T. (2001) The Inner Game of Work. Random House Trade Paperbacks. New York

Hayes, P (2006) NLP Coaching. Open University Press. McGraw Hill

Hutchinson P. and Molden, D (2008) Brilliant NLP. Pearson Prentice Hall. Harlow, England

Jackson, P and McKergrow, M (2008) The Solutions Focus. Nicholas Brealey International. London. Boston.

Martin, C. (2007) The Life Coaching Handbook. Crown House Publishing Limited

McDermott, I and Jago, W (2002) The NLP Coach. Piatkus.

McDermott, I and Jago, W (2009) The Coaching Bible. Piatkus.

McMahon, G and Archer A (2010) 101 Coaching Strategies and Techniques. Routledge. London and New York

O'Connor, J and Lages, A. (2004) Coaching with NLP. Element, An Imprintmof Harper-Collins Publishers. London

O'Donovan, G and Martin, C (2000) The Thirty Minute Life Coach. The British Coaching Academy UK Limited

Passmore, J (Ed) (2007) Excellence in Coaching: The Industry Guide. Association for Coaching. Kogan Page. London and Philadelphia

Starr, J. (2008a) Brilliant Coaching: How to be a brilliant coach in your workplace. Pearson Prentice Hall. Harlow, England

Starr, J. (2008b) The Coaching Manual. Pearson Prentice Hall Business. Harlow, England

Tracy, B. (2002) Eat that frog. Berrett-Koehler Publishers Inc. San Francisco

Tracy, B (2004) Goals! Berrett-Koehler Publishers Inc. San Francisco

Watson, A (2010) How to Succeed with NLP. Capstone

Whitmore, J. (2009) Coaching for Performance (4th Edition). Nicholas Brealey Publishing

Whitworth et al. (2009) Co-Active Coaching (2nd Edition). Davies-Black. Boston-London

Zeus, P and Skiffington, S. (2007) The Coaching at Work Toolkit. McGraw-Hill. Australia

Zeus, P and Skiffington, S. (2008) The Complete Guide to Coaching at Work. McGraw-Hill. Australia

Printed in Great Britain
by Amazon.co.uk, Ltd.,
Marston Gate.